METANOIA
The Repentance

Wanna get this bookmark?

Hop on to the last page and make one!

Reviewed by

Shaykh Ul Hadees
Qazi Muhammad Imran Sahab

Mufti Asif Qasmi Sahab

"The author's integration of Islamic teachings is seamless and compelling. By linking habits and purpose to Shariah and broader Islamic values, the book offers a deeply spiritual dimension that sets it apart from other self-help titles. This makes it particularly valuable for readers seeking guidance that is both practical and rooted in their faith."

-Qazi Muhammad Imran Sahab

Darul Uloom Bilaliya [Srinagar]

Review by Qazi Muhammad Imran Sahab:

Title: Metanoia The Repentance

The preface of this book lays out a thoughtful roadmap for readers seeking self-improvement within the framework of Islamic principles. The author begins by addressing the powerful role habits play in shaping our lives and character, drawing a clear connection between our daily actions and our long-term fulfilment. This practical exploration of habits is enhanced with strategies for identifying which ones are truly beneficial, making the content both relevant and actionable.

One of the book's standout features is its focus on aligning personal growth with finding purpose and attaining happiness. By encouraging readers to appreciate what they have and enjoy the present moment, the book fosters a positive, gratitude-centered mindset.

The author's integration of Islamic teachings is seamless and compelling. By linking habits and purpose to Shariah and broader Islamic values, the book offers a deeply spiritual dimension that sets it apart from other self-help titles. This makes it particularly valuable for readers seeking guidance that is both practical and rooted in their faith.

The structure of the book appears well-organised, moving from habits to purpose and then to a holistic application of these ideas. This progression feels natural and ensures that readers can easily follow along while reflecting on their own lives. The promise of making life
"easier and more beautiful" is both inspiring and reassuring, and the book delivers actionable wisdom to achieve this goal.

This book is an invaluable resource for the youth, equipping them with tools for personal growth and guiding them towards a balanced, fulfilling life in harmony with Islamic values. It is a mustread for anyone seeking success and peace in this world and the Hereafter.

Qazi Mohammad Imran
Darul Uloom Bilaliya

Srinagar

"Wisdom Unveiled: Islamic Habits for Success and Personal Transformation"

"Wisdom in Practice: Islamic Habits for Success and Personal Growth"

"Wisdom's Way: Islamic Habits for Success and Personal Fulfillment"

"Pathways to Success: Islamic Insights on Habits and Growth"

"Islamic Habits: Achieving Success and Inner Peace"

"Spiritual Serenity: Islamic Habits for Success and Inner Peace"

"Spiritual Success: Islamic Practices for a Fulfilling Life"

"Harmony of Faith: Islamic Habits for Success and Spiritual Growth"

"Spiritual Steps: Islamic Habits for Success and Serenity"

Metanoia
THE
REPENTANCE

Serenity and Success

Whispers of Faith

Graceful Living

Paths of Peace

"Habits Shape Character"

"Transformative Habits: Shaping Character for Success"

"Pathways to Purpose: Building Good Habits for a Better Life and Spiritual Success"

"Habits of Grace: Achieving Success Through Spiritual and Personal Growth"

"Elevated Living: Forming Good Habits for Success and Spiritual Fulfillment"

"Success Through Sacred Habits: A Guide to Better Living and Spiritual Connection"

"Holistic Habits: Achieving Success and Spiritual Harmony"

Preface

Preface

MUST READ

This book shall start by discussing habits, their influence upon our lives, and how they can elevate our character. We will go on to discuss which habits are good for us, how to find our life's purpose, and how to be happy and enjoy what we have. Then, we will integrate all those ideas in order to make our lives easier and more beautiful according to Islamic teachings and Shariah. We are also going to connect the first two chapters with Islamic teachings in order to help us find our meaning.

The fourth chapter will teach
you a game of characters where
you identify your best fit and
try to apply them in your life so
that you may hopefully change
for good. Finally, we are going
to learn from Chapter five
about the Sunnah of our
beloved Prophet ﷺ, why they
are so important, how we can
appreciate them more, and
forgotten Sunnah practices we
can apply into daily lives.
إن شاء الله, earning rewards in the
hereafter.

*O our Rabb, accept from us with goodly acceptance
and seek it grow in a good manner*

- Hatim Bin Khaleef

Hatim Bin Khaleef

Hatim Bin Khaleef, a medical student [MBBS] and practicing Muslim from Shopian, Kashmir, loves to help and guide his friends and people towards Islam with the help of Allah. He found early inspiration in books. Hatim has authored several books, including "Life Towards Allah" and "Motivational Muslims,"

*"No one of you truly believes until he loves
for his brother what he loves for himself"* [1]

*- My beloved and our leader Prophet
Muhammad* ﷺ

[1] :Al-Bukhaari (13) and Muslim (45) narrated from Anas رضي الله عنه that the Prophet (ﷺ) said: "No one of you truly
believes until he loves for his brother what he loves for himself."

In this chapter, we will discuss how habits influence a person's mind and character, and their path to success.

"HABITS SHAPE___

CHARACTER"

"Building Good Habits for a Better Life and Spiritual Success"

Healthy Habits.
HABITS: THE HIDDEN KEY TO SUCCESS

A habit is something that you do or a kind of behavior which you continuously carry on, such as saying "Bismillah" before eating or greeting others with "Assalamu Alaikum."

Some habits improve your physical, mental, and spiritual well-being, while others might have a negative impact on your daily life. However, with a little effort and consistency, you can change habits that aren't helpful and develop new ones that make your life more meaningful and rewarding.

This book is going to teach you how helpful habits can be and will also give you practical tips on breaking unhelpful habits and replacing them with simple, better ones that are good for your well-being.

HABITS VS. ROUTINES

And once you understand that habits can change, you have the freedom and the responsibility to remake them.

-Charles Duhigg

The difference between a habit and a routine is that a habit happens by itself with little to no conscious effort; routine is intentional and disciplined.

For instance, Saying "Bismillah" before the food becomes habit; whereas a routine could be consistently making dua while leaving home or sitting down to recite a few verses of the Quran before sleeping.

IS IT POSSIBLE TO LEARN NEW HABITS?

You can easily teach yourself new habits. One of the methods is called "stacking," where you pair a new habit with a habit you already have. This makes a new behavior more automatic in time.

For example, you could place a note next to your prayer mat to remind you to do dhikr after your prayers. Each time you finish your prayer, the sight of the note would cue you to do your dhikr. Soon enough, you would no longer need the note, for you would begin your dhikr habitually as soon as you finished praying.

You have to be patient with yourself since it requires practice up to approximately 66 days for something to become a habit.

Additional Expert Tips to Solidify New Habits

- **Make it Realistic:** Choose a habit that is attainable for you. The first and foremost thing about building a habit is consistency. For instance, if there is no possibility of working out for one hour, you may attempt to do it for 20 minutes instead.

- **Make it Convenient:** The easier the habit, the more chances you will follow through with it. Filling up your water bottle the night before and having it in your bag are effective ways if drinking water is your goal.

- **Practice the Same Time Each Day:** Introducing your habit at the same time each day can work wonders in establishing a habit. External cues like your journal on the nightstand can remind you to take some time before bed to write.

- **Cheer yourself on:** Celebrate small wins; it would keep you motivated. Some pep talks hung on your wall or the fridge would serve as a reminder of how you have progressed.

- **Use the Buddy System:** Working with someone who also desires the same objective keeps you both accountable. Regular check-ins will not only track your progress; it will encourage each other.

"Don't be too hard on yourself if you miss a day or two when trying to form a new habit," says Malone. Research from 2012 suggests that occasionally forgetting to perform the behavior you want to adopt usually won't prevent you from eventually forming the habit.

"Rather than seeing this as a failure, use it as an opportunity to identify the obstacle and refine your strategy," recommends Jahn.

For instance, if meditating for 20 minutes daily feels overwhelming, try reducing it to 5 minutes. If you forget to meditate, set a daily alarm on your phone as a reminder.

The Bottom Line

Habits significantly influence various aspects of your life, including mental and physical health, productivity, relationships, and self-esteem.

You can always develop new, beneficial habits and change those that no longer serve you. Remember to practice patience and self-compassion, as forming and maintaining new habits takes time.

Seeking extra support can also be beneficial. Whether you want to establish a new habit or break an old one, a therapist can provide personalized guidance and support.

"Inspired by the book 'Atomic Habits,' let's explore key points to grasp its concepts and learn practical strategies for implementation."

In Chapter 7 of "Atomic Habits," James Clear explores how to effectively change behavior by making habits less visible, an inversion of the 1st Law of Behavior Change. Once habits are ingrained, they're hard to forget.

Instead of relying on sheer willpower to resist bad habits, which is only effective in the short term, those with strong self-control simply minimize their exposure to temptation. This means spending less time in situations where bad habits are likely to occur, rather than constantly battling urges.

Key strategies from the chapter include:
1. **Habits Scorecard**: Use it to become aware of and track your current habits.
2. **Implementation Intentions and Habit Stacking**: Use these techniques to establish new habits effectively.
3. **Environment Redesign**: Make good cues more prominent and visible in your surroundings.
4. **Cue Reduction**: Minimize exposure to cues that trigger your bad habits.

By implementing these strategies, you can make positive changes to your habits by adjusting your environment and reducing the allure of bad habits.

METANOIA-THE REPENTANCE

In Chapter 11 of "Atomic Habits," James Clear explores how to achieve consistent progress in habit execution. He emphasizes that the most effective way to learn is through practice rather than extensive planning. The focus should be on the quantity of repetitions rather than the duration spent performing the habit. Clear outlines the process of habit formation as follows:

1. **Start**: Initially, a habit demands significant energy and attention to perform.
2. **Motion**: With repeated practice, the habit becomes easier but still requires some effort and attention.
3. **Automation**: Over time, the habit becomes more automatic and ingrained in behavior.

To reach the point where a habit becomes automatic, Clear introduces the concept of the "habit line," where the behavior can be performed almost effortlessly, without much conscious thought. The key takeaway is that consistent repetition of the habit is more crucial than the time spent performing it to achieve automation.

"The process of building habits is actually the process of becoming yourself."

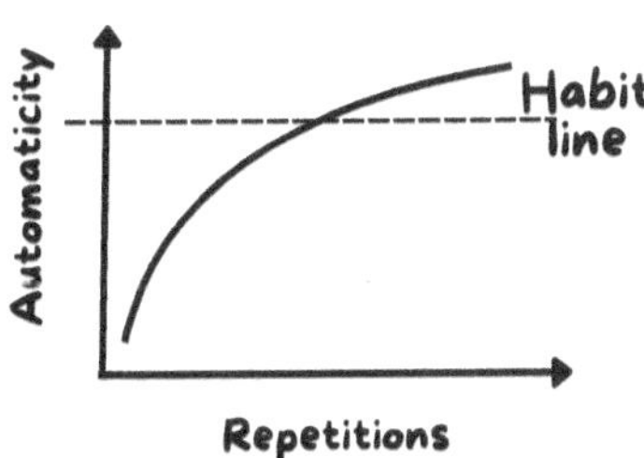

METANOIA-THE REPENTANCE

In Chapter 15 of "Atomic Habits," James Clear discusses the implementation of the Cardinal Rule of Behavior Change. This rule revolves around how our behaviors are influenced by whether we were rewarded or punished for them in the past. Clear summarizes this concept with the cardinal principles: "What is rewarded is repeated. What is punished is avoided."

While the earlier laws increase the likelihood of performing a habit in the present, the fourth law focuses on sustaining these behaviors into the future. Clear highlights a discrepancy between two types of environments:

1. **Immediate-Return Environment**: Reflecting early human societies where actions led to instant, clear outcomes.
2. **Delayed-Return Environment**: Modern societies where actions may take time to yield desired results.

Despite our brains' evolutionary heritage favoring immediate rewards, contemporary society emphasizes delayed gratification. Hence, the updated Cardinal Rule states: "What is immediately rewarded is repeated. What is immediately punished is avoided."

To make habits stick, Clear advises finding ways to introduce immediate rewards or successes as incentives for sustaining desired behaviors.

In Chapter 18 of "Atomic Habits," James Clear explores the dynamics between talent and hard work in achieving success. He suggests that maximizing your chances of success involves choosing both the right habits and the appropriate field of competition:

1. **Choosing the Right Habit**: Success comes more easily when you select habits that align with your strengths and natural inclinations.

2. **Genetic Influence**: Your genes can play a significant role in shaping your habits and behaviors, influencing your advantage or disadvantage depending on the circumstances.

To align your habits and pursuits with your personality and strengths (We will also get a deep understanding about it in next chapter), J Clear suggests employing an explore/exploit trade-off strategy. Begin with exploration to discover activities that resonate with you, asking questions such as:

- What activities are enjoyable for me but effective for others?
- When do I lose track of time?
- Where do I excel beyond average returns?
- What skills come naturally to me?

After exploration, focus on refining the most promising pursuits through experimentation and consistent effort. If you find yourself succeeding, continue to exploit those strengths. Conversely, if you encounter difficulties, revisit exploration to find a better fit or consider creating a niche that combines your interests.

Clear underscores the importance of hard work in achieving success, quoting the adage that "hard work beats talent when talent doesn't work hard." Ultimately, your genetic predispositions can guide you towards areas where your efforts are most likely to pay off.

NOTES

"In this chapter, we will explore how to find the right habits to construct a purposeful and joyful life."

†RAISON

D'ÊTRE

"reason to be."

And here's where the concept of ikigai comes into play.

Indeed, the concept of Ikigai aligns well with the discussion on finding purpose and fulfillment through your habits and endeavors. Ikigai, a Japanese term meaning "a reason for being," emphasizes the intersection of what you love, what you are good at, what the world needs, and what you can be paid for. It's about discovering that sweet spot where your passions, talents, mission, and profession converge.

In the context of habit formation and success, Ikigai encourages you to not only consider what activities align with your personality and strengths but also to explore how these can contribute positively to your life and the lives of others. It reinforces the idea that sustainable happiness and fulfillment come from engaging in activities that resonate deeply with your sense of purpose and provide a meaningful contribution to the world.

Only things that are imperfect, incomplete, and ephemeral can truly be beautiful, because only those things resemble the natural world.

METANOIA-THE REPENTANCE

HOW TO USE THE IKIGAI DIAGRAM TO FIND YOUR PURPOSE

"Ikigai," which loosely translates to "the reason for being" or "the reason you wake up in the morning." It is believed that each person has their own unique ikigai, a profound quest that defines their life's purpose and calling.

Initially, you might dismiss this as a lofty idea that sounds good in theory but isn't practical. Indeed, the popular Venn diagram representation of ikigai in Western interpretations doesn't fully capture its true essence. However, there are valuable lessons to be learned from this concept that shouldn't be overlooked.

In essence, I view ikigai as an idealistic pursuit. It's rare to find a single activity that perfectly aligns with all aspects depicted in the Venn diagram. Those who solely chase after their ikigai may spend a lifetime in search of it, mistakenly believing that without discovering it, they cannot lead a meaningful and fulfilling life.

The reality is, fulfillment can be found through various activities and pursuits that resonate deeply with us. We can derive satisfaction from multiple sources and approach our purpose from different angles. Rather than fixating on finding one singular ikigai, it's more productive to explore and engage in meaningful activities that bring us joy and fulfillment.

The ikigai Venn diagram provides a powerful framework for thinking about how to spend your time. The most important lessons are as follows:
1. Don't neglect any of the circles.
2. Aim for the intersections.

BALANCE

Lesson 1st is really about finding balance. If you neglect any of the circles, you're likely to feel dissatisfied.

For example, if you focus only on one circle, like work for money alone, you might seem successful on the outside but feel deeply unhappy inside. Think of a workaholic who never enjoys life, doesn't use their strengths, and doesn't contribute to their community.

Even if you satisfy three circles but ignore the fourth, you may still feel like something's missing. For instance, you might have a fulfilling career that you excel at, but if it doesn't fulfill a greater purpose or help others, you might feel a psychological emptiness that volunteering or giving back could help fill.

METANOIA-THE REPENTANCE

OVERLAP IS GOOD

Lesson 2nd emphasizes the importance of aiming for the intersections where these circles overlap. It's beneficial to spend your time and energy in these areas.

For instance, if your job aligns with your strengths, you'll likely find greater job satisfaction. Similarly, improving your skills in something you're passionate about can enhance your enjoyment of that activity. You can also integrate your hobbies into community contributions; for example, coaching a local Little League team if you enjoy playing baseball.

When faced with job choices that both meet financial needs, opting for the one that fulfills a significant societal need can provide greater personal fulfillment.

While very few people discover a singular ikigai, many find activities that almost fulfill this ideal, residing at the intersection of two or three circles. These pursuits can often be fulfilling enough to lead a satisfying life..

METANOIA-THE REPENTANCE

Three Classic Mistakes

The ikigai diagram also highlights the pitfalls of three common mistakes:

1. **Spending too much time on just one thing**: While focusing intensely on one pursuit can lead to mastery, it's risky to rely solely on it. For instance, dedicating all your time to a beloved art form might not guarantee a sustainable career. Similarly, focusing solely on a favorite sport could lead to setbacks like injuries. Diversifying your interests can prevent over-reliance on a single activity and provide alternative sources of fulfillment and resilience.

2. **Believing life should have only one purpose**: It's unnecessarily restrictive to limit yourself to a single life purpose. Embracing multiple passions often enriches life and can have positive impacts on the world. For example, Steve Martin, known for his acting career, also thrives as a stand-up comedian and banjo player. Bill Gates, originally a software developer, now channels his efforts into philanthropy through the Bill & Melinda Gates Foundation.

3. **Spreading yourself too thin by doing too many things**: Engaging in numerous activities may prevent you from achieving excellence in any one area. Being a jack of all trades might mean you're proficient in various fields but not exceptional in any, potentially limiting career advancement and financial reward.

In essence, balancing your pursuits and interests allows for both depth and diversity in life, fostering fulfillment and resilience across various endeavors.

"Thus we have a paradoxical situation: On the job people feel skillful and challenged, and therefore feel more happy, strong, creative, and satisfied. In their free time people feel that there is generally not much to do and their skills are not being used, and therefore they tend to feel more sad, weak, dull, and dissatisfied. Yet they would like to work less and spend more time in leisure."

METANOIA-THE REPENTANCE

CENTRE OF THE DIAGRAM

Now, let's delve into the concept of "searching" for your ikigai. In Western terms, this equates to "finding your passion." Many self-help experts and career advisors advocate for discovering and pursuing your passion as the key to fulfillment. However, this advice overlooks several critical realities.

Firstly, it assumes that everyone has a singular true calling that can meet both financial and psychological needs. Secondly, it presumes that once you identify your passion, circumstances will allow you to pursue it freely. Lastly, it suggests that introspection alone can reveal your true passion.

In reality, while some individuals may stumble upon their ikigai through reflection, it's more commonly developed through persistent effort and hard work. Sometimes, your passion may align with a viable career path, but other times it may not. If what you love isn't in demand or if you lack the necessary skills, you'll need to invest time and effort to become employable. During this process, you may need to support yourself through other means while pursuing your passion on the side.

In essence, having a passionate aspiration isn't sufficient; dedication and hard work are crucial factors in achieving your dreams.

As Steve Martin advised aspiring comedians, success often comes from honing your skills until you excel to the point where opportunities cannot be ignored: "Be so good they can't ignore you."

My thoughts on IKIGAI

Currently, I am a medical student deeply engaged in both offline and online dawah activities, alongside acquiring knowledge from scholars of Islam. My fascination lies in understanding the intricacies of the human body and its functions. However, alongside this medical pursuit, I feel a profound calling to engage in dawah, inviting people to Islam and guiding them towards the path of truth.

Teaching, leading, and writing have always been passions of mine, though initially, I lacked the skill to earn from them. Initially, I focused solely on what I loved, residing in the top circle of the diagram.

Through consistent practice and dedication, I have significantly improved in both my leading and preaching abilities, transforming these interests into passions. I aimed to intersect these pursuits on the diagram and diligently worked towards achieving that goal.

The ikigai diagram can sometimes give the impression that you're limited to just one true calling, but that's not necessarily true.

Since childhood, I've always been eager to lead, to assist others, and to guide them. However, in my field of study, this seemed impractical. By aligning with my earlier ikigai, as I mentioned before, I discovered a path to my new ikigai—establishing my own dawah gathering. Here, we discuss and learn form each other and I usually have a job to maintain it and run it properly, which is why I find deep fulfillment in my work today.
—and thats how I found my another ikigai.

Life is finite, so you can't pursue everything, but you can cultivate multiple passions that align with societal needs. By excelling in these pursuits, you can turn them into meaningful work that supports your livelihood.

METANOIA-THE REPENTANCE

VALUE THE LIFE

Finally, the ikigai model overlooks several crucial aspects.

One such aspect is social relationships. A truly fulfilling and joyful life cannot be attained without nurturing meaningful connections with others. Therefore, it's essential not to become so absorbed in the pursuit of ikigai that you overlook the importance of maintaining relationships with friends and family.

Life is not a problem to be solved. Just remember to have something that keeps you busy doing what you love while being surrounded by the people who love you

Enjoying or creating beauty is free, and something all humans have access to

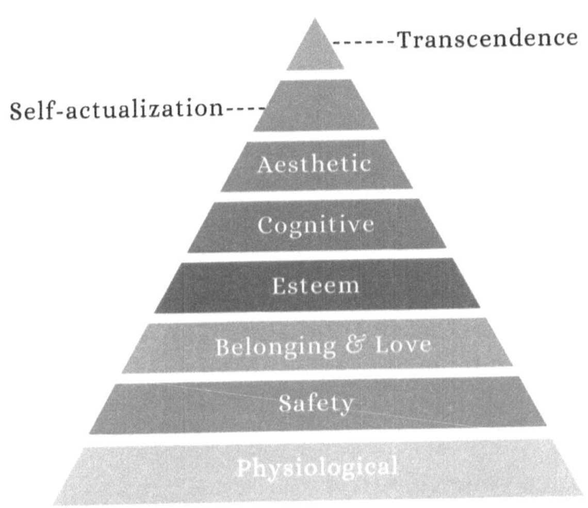

The pursuit of ikigai is really about self-actualizing; it's about the top of the pyramid. So if you want to satisfy your ikigai circles, you'll first need to build a strong foundation, and that means establishing healthy habits.

1. Morality, creativity,spontaneity, problem solving, lack of prejudice, acceptance of facts.
2. Self-esteem, confidence, achievement, respect of others, respect by others.
3. Friendship, family, sexual intimacy.
4. Security of body, of employment, of resources, of morality, of the family, of health, of property.
5. Breathing, food, water, sleep, homeostasis, excretion.

METANOIA-THE REPENTANCE

FIND YOUR WAY OF LIFE

It's important to understand the four elements of ikigai to help you uncover your life's purpose.

1. Unveil your passion

Passions are the activities that make time fly by and cause you to feel excited and alive. It's what you enjoy doing most, and, perhaps something you'd do even if you weren't getting paid for it.

2. Recognize your vocation

Your skills and strengths are those things that you naturally excel at that might not come as easily to others. Perhaps you're skilled in math, writing, or creating music. Identifying your vocation is another way of tapping into your special skills that deserve recognition.

3. Discover your mission

This element of ikigai helps you explore the needs of the world and where you can make a difference. Are there problems or challenges in your community or in the world you feel passionate about solving? Identify them. There's your mission.

4. Cultivate your profession

Your profession is where you look at how to make a living from your passion and mission. For example, if you're a talented painter who believes the world would be a better place if more individuals could express their creativity through painting. Consider starting to teach painting lessons. Transforming your passion and mission into your career may require some time to evolve. Have faith in the journey.

THE REAL MISSION

Every soul will taste death. And you will only receive your full reward on the Day of Judgment. Whoever is spared from the Fire and is admitted into Paradise will 'indeed' triumph, whereas the life of this world is no more than the delusion of enjoyment.

Quran 3:185

After learning the concepts from the previous two chapters on habit formation and identifying beneficial habits, let's now merge these ideas with our Islamic viewpoint. Let's visualize how these habits can enhance our lives, aiming for happiness and ultimate success in the Hereafter, which defines true success.

Let's merge the Chapter 1 &
Chapter 2 into our Islamic
perspective....

THE
REAL___

MISSION
"AKHIRAH"

You've been on this Earth for many years now, and in that time you've experienced the full spectrum of human emotion. You've known the depths of sorrow and the heights of happiness. You've built relationships with people who have touched your heart in ways words can hardly describe.

Yet, you often find yourself pondering the true purpose of it all. Is this really it? Were you created simply to find a job, earn a living, raise a family, and then watch as the cycle repeats, your family tree growing ever larger?

In reflecting on your own journey, you see the milestones—achievements that once seemed monumental but now blend into the tapestry of your life. And the losses, those sharp pains of regret and grief, they too have shaped you, leaving scars that tell stories of battles fought and lessons learned.

Each day, you strive to understand the deeper meaning behind your existence. Is it merely about survival and reproduction, or is there something more profound waiting to be discovered? This question, perhaps, is the essence of your human quest—a search for meaning in a world that often seems to blur the lines between the ordinary and the extraordinary.

At some point in our lives, we all wonder about the meaning of life and why we were created. Many people spend their entire lives searching for this answer. Islam provides a clear answer to this question. Let's explore a brief discussion on this topic.

Any sane person would agree that everything created has a creator and a specific purpose. For example, vehicles help us with transportation, our ears help us hear, and our eyes help us see. One of the names of Allah is Al-Hakeem (The All-Wise), so it makes sense to understand that Allah created us, not in vain, but with a true purpose. This is mentioned in many verses in ..the Qur'an

'And We did not create the heaven and earth and that between them in play.' [Surah Al-Anbiya 21:16]

'Did you then think that We had created you without **purpose**, and that you would never be returned to Us?'
[Surah Al-Muminoon 23:115]

Similarly, when we think deeply about the question, human beings are created with favors far better than animals. Hence, we can say that humans are not created merely to eat, drink and reproduce. But there are people who are ignorant and are on the path of disbelief that they deny the true wisdom behind creation, and only care about enjoying the pleasures of this world. Allah describes the life of such people as that of the animals

'...As for the disbelievers, they enjoy themselves and feed like cattle...' [Surah Muhammad 47:12]
'Let them eat and enjoy themselves and be diverted by [false] hope, for they are going to know.' [Surah Al-Hijr 15:3]

So, why were humans created? Allah is the one who made us, and He understands the purpose behind our creation. Allah has explained that the heavens, the earth, life, and death were all created to test us, and this test includes humans too. Those who obey Allah will be rewarded, while those who disobey will be punished.

'...that He might test you as to which of you is best in deed...' [Surah Hud 11:7]

Another key reason for our creation is to recognize His oneness (Tawhid) and to worship Him alone, without associating any partners with Him.

'And I did not create the jinn and mankind except to worship Me.'
[Surah Ad-Dhariyat 51:56]

METANOIA-THE REPENTANCE

Inborn Propensity [Fitrat]

Allah took an oath from all the descendants of Adam (AS) before they were born. He gathered them, generation after generation, and addressed all the souls directly, making them bear witness that He was their Lord. This oath is imprinted on every soul before it enters the fetus, resulting in a child being born with a natural belief in the oneness of Allah. This state of belief is known as Fitrah.

"And remember when your Lord brought forth from the loins of the children of Adam their descendants and had them testify regarding themselves. Allah asked, 'Am I not your Lord?' They replied, 'Yes, You are! We testify.' He cautioned, 'Now you have no right to say on Judgment Day, "We were not aware of this."'" [Surah Al-Araf 7:172]

Every person has the seed of oneness sown in their heart at birth. This belief can be either reinforced or dampened by social conditioning. If a child were left alone, it would naturally grow to believe in the oneness of Allah, but environmental influences play a huge role.

Allah's Messenger ﷺ said, "No child is born but has the Islamic Faith, but its parents turn it into a Jew or a Christian…" [Sahih Al-Bukhari 6599, 6600]

Worshipping Allah ﷻ

In Islam, worship is defined as 'obedient submission to the will of Allah.' This means that every created being submits to its Creator by following the physical laws established by Him.

"And to Him belong all those in the heavens and the earth—all are subject to His Will." [Surah Ar-Room 30:26]

The obedience to divine laws demonstrated by the Prophets sent by Allah forms the foundation of worship in Islam. Whoever submits to Allah and follows His commands will find success, while those who turn away from His divine commands will face loss. Ultimately, all people will be gathered in the hereafter where Allah will reward or punish them according to their deeds.

Allah mentions how the polytheists deny the rewards or punishments:

"But if you were to say to them, 'You shall indeed be raised up after death,' those who disbelieve would be sure to say, 'This is nothing but obvious magic.'" [Surah Hood 11:7]

Islam provides the answer to the search for the meaning of life. The purpose of the creation of all men and women throughout all times is singular: to know and worship Allah. Our universe and all its elements operate in harmony by adhering to the physical laws set by Allah, the Supreme Creator. Only when humans worship Allah, submitting to Him and His divine laws, can they achieve peace and harmony in their lives and the hope for heaven. Without the hope for heaven, life loses its ultimate value and purpose.

Productivity Through the Lens of Eternity
[Embracing the Hereafter]

'Umar رضي الله عنه , a notable leader, prioritized the Hereafter throughout his life. He believed that this worldly life is temporary, and preparing for the eternal Afterlife should be the primary focus. He emphasized that striving for Paradise and avoiding Hellfire motivates believers differently, guiding them closer to Allah. 'Umar رضي الله عنه's advice centered on focusing on personal integrity over public image, ensuring sincerity in faith. His final sermon urged people to prioritize spiritual gains over worldly pursuits, emphasizing accountability to Allah in the Hereafter.

We can understand some points below

- Eternal Happiness through Spiritual Growth: Prioritizing spiritual growth and righteousness leads to lasting happiness in the Hereafter.
- Accountability to Allah: Believers are motivated by understanding they will be held accountable by Allah. Belief in Paradise and Hellfire guides actions towards pleasing Allah and avoiding sins.
- Sincerity and Integrity: True piety is shown not just through public actions but also through sincere faith and integrity in personal conduct.
- Awareness of Life's Transience: Recognizing the fleeting nature of worldly life and the certainty of death prompts believers to focus on deeds that benefit them in the Hereafter.
- Guidance and Wisdom: Seeking advice and guidance from knowledgeable individuals helps maintain a righteous path in life.

Belief in the Hereafter holds profound significance in Islam and serves as a catalyst for true productivity. Some may question the purpose of striving and setting goals in a fleeting world that ends in death. This perspective often leads to a sense of nihilism, **wasting away the potential of life.**

Contrastingly, embracing the belief in an everlasting life after this one, filled with eternal bliss and happiness, motivates individuals to pursue higher purposes and nobler goals. Whether or not we witness the fruition of our efforts in our lifetime becomes secondary; what matters is leaving behind enduring projects that continue to benefit others long after we're gone.

Islam emphasizes engaging in projects that have lasting impacts beyond our earthly existence. Such endeavors include charitable acts, knowledge that enriches lives, and raising righteous children who pray for our well-being. Prophet Muhammad ﷺ highlighted this eternal perspective, stating, "When a person dies, their deeds come to an end except for three: ongoing charity, beneficial knowledge, or a righteous child who prays for them."

These teachings encourage believers to look beyond immediate gains and invest in legacies that yield continuous rewards, even centuries after their departure from this world.

Elevating Goals

Belief in the Hereafter compels us to think on a grander scale, extending our vision beyond our lifetime to consider the lasting impact we can leave. In Islam, the concept of the Hereafter encourages a profound reflection on the consequences of our actions. It prompts believers to look beyond immediate needs and desires, directing their aspirations toward goals that transcend this temporal existence.

When we internalize the belief in an Afterlife, our motivations shift. No longer driven solely by the fleeting rewards of this world, our focus shifts to the enduring rewards of the next. This perspective imbues everything we do with a spiritual depth, elevating our goals and efforts to a higher plane.

Moreover, belief in the Afterlife fosters greater adherence to principles. It strengthens our resolve to uphold these principles even in challenging circumstances, knowing that our ultimate accountability lies in the Hereafter. This steadfast commitment to ethical conduct reflects a deep-seated faith that guides our actions towards righteousness and perseverance in the face of trials.

As we read these three chapters, a profound understanding emerges regarding the significance of habits. And not just any habits, but those that are beneficial to our spiritual growth and aligned with preparing for the Hereafter. This shift in focus moves us away from the fake pleasures of worldly life towards a mindset for eternal bliss. By cultivating habits that serve our ultimate goal of attaining Paradise, we start a journey of transformation. This new mentality ensures our actions are not just for the present, but for an everlasting reward in the Hereafter.
And thats what I call "METANOIA - The Repentance."

"STRENGTH ISN'T JUST ABOUT PHYSIQUE; IT'S ABOUT THE MINDSET. PEOPLE WITH PHYSICAL STRENGTH SERVE, BUT THOSE WITH MENTAL STRENGTH LEAD."

- Hatim Bin Khaleef

"SIT WITH THOSE WHO HAVE SINNED AND REPENTED FOR THEY HAVE THE SOFTEST OF HEARTS."

- Umar ibn Al-Khattab

Lets play a game designed by Me (Hatim Bin Khaleef) called "Persona Pathways" it is a game that suggests a journey or adventure where you create and develop your characters by choosing specific traits. The word "Persona" implies the character's personality or identity, while "Pathways" indicates various routes or choices that players can take to shape their characters' traits and abilities. Together, it conveys a dynamic and exploratory experience in character development.

PERSONA

PATHWAYS

STARTED

I'm going to share some examples of different types of people and their characteristics for you to reflect on and apply to your own life. Whether you're interested in leadership, moral guidance, or simply becoming a better person, these traits can serve as a blueprint for personal growth.

First, familiarize yourself with all these traits, as each plays a crucial role in becoming a better person. As you continue, concentrate on the traits that resonate most with you and commit to cultivating them. Through consistent practice over 2 to 3 months, you'll observe these qualities becoming integral to your character. Whether your goal is to lead others, inspire through words, or simply live well and be a good person, integrating these traits into your daily life will steadily shape your character into one that you want to become.

"Remind yourselves of God, for it is
a cure. Do not remind yourselves of
the people, for it is a disease."
- Umar ibn Al-Khattab

01
HEALING
&
KINDNESS

Kindness is a flower of Islam, teaching us the importance of treating everyone with respect and compassion. When we show kindness to our parents and family members, we strengthen our most important relationships, creating a loving and supportive environment. Acts of charity, when coupled with kind words and gestures, not only help those in need but also spread positivity and warmth. Emulating Allah's mercy and compassion through our kindness ennobles us. By being kind, we contribute to a selfless, compassionate society that fosters resilience and social stability. This, in turn, brings us a sense of peace and happiness, knowing that we are making the world a better place for everyone involved.

Healing others through kindness is a profound act that transcends mere gestures. By extending compassion, empathy, and support to those in need, we not only alleviate their immediate pain or suffering but also contribute to their emotional and spiritual well-being. Kindness has a remarkable power to heal wounds, mend broken spirits, and restore faith in humanity. Whether through a comforting word, a helping hand, or a heartfelt gesture, each act of kindness creates a ripple effect of positivity, fostering a sense of connection and belonging.

Ultimately, healing through kindness not only enriches the lives of others but also nurtures our own souls, reaffirming the beauty of human kindness and its transformative impact on both giver and receiver.

Once again, I urge you to not just read but also implement these principles. Following through is crucial for seeing real change. Take action and apply these teachings to make a meaningful difference in your life and the lives of others.

- **Smile and Greet Others:** Start each interaction with a genuine smile and a warm greeting.

- **Listen Actively:** Practice active listening when someone is talking to you, showing genuine interest in their thoughts and feelings.

- **Express Gratitude:** Regularly express gratitude to others for their kindness, support, or even for small favors.

- **Offer Help:** Be proactive in offering help to those in need, whether it's carrying groceries, assisting with tasks, or offering your skills.

- **Show Compassion:** Approach others' problems or challenges with empathy and offer support without judgment.

- **Share Your Knowledge:** Share your expertise or knowledge with others who can benefit from it.

- **Donate or Volunteer:** Contribute to charitable causes or volunteer your time to help those less fortunate.

- **Give Genuine Compliments:** Notice and acknowledge the positive qualities or efforts of others with sincere compliments.

- **Practice Patience:** Be patient with others, especially in challenging situations, and avoid unnecessary criticism.

- **Forgive and Let Go:** Practice forgiveness and let go of grudges or resentments towards others.

- **Support Someone's Dreams:** Encourage and support someone in pursuing their goals or dreams.

- **Be Polite and Respectful:** Treat everyone with politeness and respect, regardless of differences.

- **Take Care of the Environment:** Practice eco-friendly habits and encourage others to do the same.

- **Offer Words of Encouragement:** Offer words of encouragement to someone who is feeling down or facing challenges.

- **Spend Quality Time:** Dedicate quality time with loved ones, showing them that you value their presence.

- **Educate Yourself:** Educate yourself on social issues and advocate for positive change in your community.

- **Be Kind to Yourself:** Practice self-care and self-compassion, treating yourself with the same kindness you show others.

- **Celebrate Others' Success:** Celebrate the achievements and successes of others genuinely and without envy.

- **Spread Joy:** Share laughter, positivity, and joy wherever you go, uplifting the spirits of those around you.

METANOIA-THE REPENTANCE

Sometimes it takes only one act of kindness
and caring to change a person's life."
– Jackie Chan

Sabr, or patience, holds profound importance in Islam, offering resilience that can significantly ease life's challenges and foster happiness. By embodying sabr, individuals develop resilience to endure hardships with grace and steadfastness. This virtue not only strengthens character but also cultivates inner peace and spiritual growth. Through patience, one learns to navigate difficulties calmly, enhancing their ability to maintain positive relationships and pursue personal goals effectively. Ultimately, embracing sabr leads to a more fulfilling life enriched by faith, resilience, and contentment.

- **Regular Prayer:** Establishing regular prayers helps maintain spiritual connection and strengthens patience.

- **Gratitude Practice:** Cultivating gratitude for blessings counters negativity and fosters contentment.

- **Dhikr (Remembrance of Allah):** Regular remembrance of Allah through dhikr brings peace and mindfulness.

- **Seeking Knowledge:** Continuous learning and seeking beneficial knowledge deepen understanding and resilience.

METANOIA-THE REPENTANCE

- **Recitation of Qur'an:** Regular recitation and reflection on the Qur'an enhance spiritual strength.

- **Helping Others:** Acts of kindness and charity promote empathy and positivity.

- **Self-Reflection:** Regular introspection helps in identifying areas for improvement and growth.

- **Physical Exercise:** Maintaining physical health contributes to mental well-being and stamina.

- **Patience in Difficulties:** Enduring trials with patience strengthens character and trust in Allah's plan.

- **Avoiding Anger:** Controlling anger and responding calmly improve relationships and personal peace.

- **Forgiving Others:** Practicing forgiveness frees the heart from bitterness and promotes healing.

- **Being Generous:** Generosity with wealth, time, and words fosters goodwill and inner satisfaction.

- **Avoiding Gossip:** Refraining from gossip and negative talk preserves harmony and positive energy.

- **Managing Stress:** Developing coping mechanisms and seeking help when needed builds resilience.

- **Setting Realistic Goals:** Establishing achievable goals fosters a sense of accomplishment and purpose.

- **Building Relationships:** Investing in meaningful relationships provides support and joy.

- **Practicing Sabr in Daily Life:** Applying patience in daily challenges improves decision-making and peace of mind.

- **Being Mindful:** Practicing mindfulness enhances awareness and reduces stress.

- **Seeking Allah's Guidance:** Turning to Allah in prayer and supplication strengthens faith and resolves uncertainties, providing clarity and peace of mind through His divine wisdom and mercy.

- **Seeking Community:** Engaging with a supportive community provides encouragement and shared values.

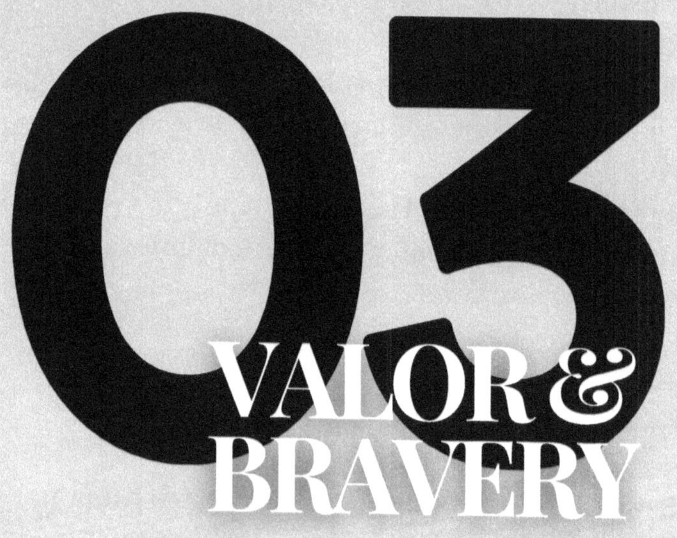
03
VALOR &
BRAVERY

Bravery in Islam encompasses both physical courage and moral strength. It involves having the fortitude to face challenges, uphold truth, and defend justice despite adversity. This virtue is exemplified in the life of Prophet Muhammad ﷺ, who endured various hardships yet remained steadfast in spreading the message of Islam. The Quran and Hadith emphasize the importance of speaking the truth even in the presence of unjust rulers, highlighting the necessity of moral courage in upholding Islamic principles. Throughout history, from the companions of the Prophet ﷺ to scholars and ordinary Muslims, bravery has been displayed in standing firm against opposition, whether verbal attacks, physical harm, or societal pressure. Courage in Islam isn't just about confronting external threats but also about internal resilience, steadfastness in faith, and enduring hardships with patience and trust in Allah. It serves as a reminder that true bravery lies in submitting to Allah's will and striving for righteousness, regardless of the challenges faced.

For this character, you can also see the renowned Islamic personality known as "The Sword of Allah," Khalid Bin Walid.

- **Seek Knowledge:** Educate yourself about Islamic teachings, values, and principles, which provide a solid foundation for courage and righteousness.

- **Strengthen Faith:** Deepen your faith in Allah (SWT) and His guidance through regular prayers, Quranic recitation, and remembrance (dhikr).

- **Understand Truth:** Clearly understand what constitutes truth and falsehood according to Islamic teachings and strive to uphold the truth in all situations.

- **Follow the Prophetic Example:** Study the life of Prophet Muhammad ﷺ and learn how He ﷺ demonstrated courage in conveying the message of Islam despite facing immense opposition.

- **Stand Firm in Beliefs:** Be unwavering in your beliefs and values, rooted in the understanding that Islam offers the ultimate truth and guidance for all aspects of life.

- **Practice Patience:** Develop patience and perseverance in the face of adversity, knowing that enduring hardships for the sake of Allah is a form of bravery.

- **Speak Up for Justice:** Courageously speak out against injustice and oppression, regardless of the consequences, knowing that justice is central to Islamic teachings.

- **Avoid Cowardice:** Reject cowardice and fear that hinder you from standing up for what is right and defending the principles of Islam.

- **Educate Others:** Share your knowledge and understanding of Islam with humility and wisdom, inviting others to embrace truth and righteousness.

- **Seek Allah's Help:** Rely on Allah's guidance and seek His assistance through supplication (dua) and sincere trust (tawakkul) in all endeavors.

- **Face Challenges with Grace:** Approach challenges with grace and dignity, reflecting the noble character and conduct advocated by Islam.

- **Learn from Historical Examples:** Study the stories of the Prophet's companions and other righteous predecessors who exemplified bravery in defending Islam.

- **Reject Compromise:** Refuse to compromise Islamic principles or dilute the truth in response to pressure or opposition, maintaining integrity in all circumstances.

- **Promote Goodness:** Actively promote goodness and virtue in society, striving to be a positive influence and role model for others.

- **Remain Resilient:** Develop resilience to setbacks and difficulties, understanding that trials are tests from Allah and opportunities to strengthen faith.

- **Cultivate Courage in Daily Life:** Practice small acts of bravery in everyday situations, such as standing up for justice, speaking honestly, and defending the oppressed.

- **Stay Informed**: Stay informed about current issues affecting Muslims globally and locally, and take informed action to support causes aligned with Islamic values.

- **Seek Support from Community**: Build a supportive network of like-minded individuals who encourage and reinforce your commitment to Islamic principles.

- **Continuous Self-Reflection:** Regularly reflect on your actions and intentions, seeking improvement and guidance from Allah to remain steadfast on the path of truth.

- **Trust in Allah's Plan:** Finally, trust in Allah's plan and His wisdom, knowing that He is the ultimate Protector and Helper of those who strive sincerely in His cause.

These points aim to guide you in developing the courage and strength needed to stand against falsehood and uphold the principles of Islam with conviction and integrity.

04
MODESTY & HAYA

Hayā in Islam holds profound significance, encompassing modesty, humility, and a sense of shame that guides behavior and interactions. It serves as a moral compass, guiding individuals to uphold dignity and respect in all aspects of life. By embodying haya, Muslims cultivate a sense of inner purity and righteousness, fostering sincerity in their actions and relationships. This virtue beautifies life by promoting humility before God and others, fostering harmony within communities, and nurturing a clear vision focused on spiritual growth and moral integrity. Hayā encourages adherence to ethical values and principles, shaping a life characterized by integrity, empathy, and a deep connection to faith, thus enriching personal fulfillment and societal well-being.

- **Reflect on the importance of hayā:** Understand that hayā is integral to spiritual growth and personal integrity.

- **Study the teachings of Prophet Muhammad (ﷺ):** Learn from his example of modesty in all aspects of life.

- **Cultivate self-awareness:** Regularly reflect on your thoughts, actions, and intentions.

- **Practice humility:** Acknowledge your strengths and weaknesses without arrogance or self-deprecation.

- **Develop a sense of decency:** Uphold modest behavior in dress, speech, and interactions.

- **Respect boundaries:** Be mindful of personal and social boundaries in all interactions.

- **Prioritize sincerity:** Strive for sincerity in your intentions and actions.

- **Avoid seeking attention:** Focus on contributing positively without seeking recognition.

- **Seek knowledge:** Continuously learn and apply Islamic teachings on modesty.

- **Be mindful of Allah:** Remember Allah's presence and strive to please Him in all actions.

- **Practice gratitude:** Appreciate blessings with humility and gratitude.

- **Seek forgiveness:** Humbly repent for shortcomings and seek Allah's forgiveness.

- **Serve others:** Help and support others with a humble heart.

- **Be gentle**: Approach conflicts and disagreements with gentleness and patience.

- **Avoid boasting:** Refrain from boasting about achievements or possessions.

- **Listen attentively:** Practice active listening and respect others' viewpoints.

- **Stay grounded**: Maintain perspective on material possessions and worldly success.

- **Associate with humble people:** Surround yourself with individuals who embody modesty and humility.

- **Monitor your intentions:** Regularly check your intentions to ensure they align with Islamic values.

- **Pray for guidance:** Turn to Allah in prayer for strength and guidance in cultivating modesty.

05
ADAPTABILITY,
JUSTICE
& LEADERSHIP

In Islam, a leader, referred to as an Imam, should embody qualities such as knowledge, power, justice, patience, and humility, drawing guidance from the Quran and Sunnah. Leadership is viewed as a responsibility rather than a position of authority. A leader must possess Taqwa (God-consciousness), honesty, and a trustworthy character, and should prioritize the welfare of the community, ensuring justice and equality for all, regardless of differences. The leader should also be empathetic, fair, and capable of understanding and addressing the needs of the people. By upholding Islamic principles, a leader can unify the community, promote peace, and ensure the well-being and security of all citizens, including non-Muslims. Effective leadership in Islam is about serving others and seeking Allah's guidance in all matters. Today, these principles can be applied to leadership roles at work, in groups, and in various settings, ensuring that we follow the teachings of the Quran and Sunnah to be just, empathetic, and effective leaders in all aspects of life.

Before moving forward lets read a short paragraph about Umar Ibn Al Khattab رضي الله عنه.

*The best person and leader to look for and seek guidance is our Prophet our beloved Sayyidina Muhammad ﷺ *

A good leader like Umar ibn Al-Khattab رضي الله عنه i vital for a community because he embodies vision, accountability, and humility. His balanced approac to leadership, combining public duty with personal growth, ensures resilience and sound decision-making. Umar's dedication to justice, regardless of personal ties or status, prevents corruption and fosters public trust. His personal engagement with the people allows for effective governance, addressing real issues. Justice is essential for social stability, equality, and protection of rights. It fosters trust, prevents abuse of power, and ensures peace and harmony. Thus, a leader who prioritizes justice and service like Umar رضي الله عنه creates a foundation for a prosperous and harmonious society.

"He who does not live in the way of his beliefs starts to believe in the way he lives."
— Umar ibn Al-Khattab

- **Knowledge and Wisdom:** A leader should have profound knowledge and wisdom to guide the community effectively.

- **Taqwa (God-consciousness):** Maintaining a deep awareness of Allah to prevent wrongdoings.

- **Justice:** Ensuring fairness and equality in all decisions and actions.

- **Patience:** Demonstrating patience in all situations, especially during challenges.

- **Humility:** Being humble and not arrogant in interactions with others.

- **Empathy and Compassion:** Showing genuine care and understanding for the needs and feelings of others.

- **Trustworthiness:** Being honest and reliable in all dealings.

- **Effective Communication:** Clearly and transparently conveying messages without ambiguity.

- **Vision:** Having a forward-thinking approach to lead the community towards future prosperity.

- **Responsibility:** Taking accountability for actions and decisions without blaming others.

- **Courage:** Facing challenges and making difficult decisions with confidence and bravery.

- **Servant Leadership:** Prioritizing the needs of others and serving the community selflessly.

- **Sound Judgment:** Making informed and wise decisions based on knowledge and insight.

- **Teamwork:** Collaborating effectively with others and recognizing the importance of followers.

- **Piety:** Maintaining a strong sense of devotion and righteousness.

- **Fair Treatment:** Ensuring that everyone, regardless of religion, race, or gender, receives equal treatment.

- **Protection and Security:** Safeguarding the community from external threats and ensuring safety.

- **Welfare Support:** Providing for the needs of the community, especially during difficult times.

- **Destroying Social Divides:** Promoting unity and eliminating divisions based on caste, religion, or gender.

- **Adherence to Islamic Principles:** Leading by example through strict adherence to the teachings of the Quran and Sunnah.

- **Listening to Others**: Valuing and considering everyone's suggestions and feedback, just as Umar ibn Al-Khattab did, to make informed and inclusive decisions.

These principles, derived from Islamic teachings, can be applied to modern leadership roles in various settings to ensure just and effective leadership.

06
GUIDANCE &
PREACHING

Preaching holds profound importance in Islam as it
serves both spiritual and worldly purposes. It is a
fundamental duty for Muslims to spread the
message of Islam with wisdom, compassion, and
sincerity, guided by Quranic teachings and the
example of Prophet Muhammad ﷺ. Through
preaching, Muslims aim to invite others to the path
of righteousness, promote understanding, and foster
a society based on justice, peace, and moral values.
This effort transcends boundaries, aiming to benefit
humanity at large by promoting universal principles
of kindness, respect, and spiritual enlightenment. In
a world where misunderstandings and conflicts
often arise from ignorance or misrepresentation,
sincere and knowledgeable preaching helps bridge
gaps, foster mutual respect, and promote harmony
among diverse communities, ultimately
contributing to a more compassionate and just
global society.

- **Begin with Supplication:** Start every effort with
  sincere prayers, seeking Allah's guidance and
  blessings.

- **Seek Spiritual Guidance:** Regularly seek prayers
  and supplications from the Khalifa for added
  spiritual strength.

- **Wisdom and Good Exhortation:** Follow the Quranic guidance to preach with wisdom, using gentle and compelling arguments.

- **Study and Preparation:** Be well-prepared with knowledge of Islamic teachings and scriptures t effectively communicate them.

- **Adapt to Context:** Tailor your message to the audience and situation, addressing relevant issues and concerns.

- **Respect and Kindness:** Approach all interaction with respect and kindness, respecting differing beliefs and opinions.

- **Personal Example:** Embody Islamic values in your own life to serve as a positive example of the faith.

- **Patience and Persistence:** Understand that preaching can be gradual and requires patience; persevere through challenges.

- **Use of Media:** Utilize various media platforms and channels to reach a wider audience and address misconceptions about Islam.

- **Dialogue and Discussion:** Engage in meaningful conversations, actively listening to understand others' perspectives.

- **Personalized Approach:** Tailor your approach based on individual circumstances and intellectual levels.

- **Empathy and Understanding:** Show empathy towards others' concerns and challenges, addressing them with compassion.

- **Highlight Practicality:** Emphasize the practical aspects of Islamic teachings and their relevance to contemporary issues.

- **Address Misconceptions:** Clarify misunderstandings about Islam through factual explanations and examples.

- **Utilize Opportunities:** Be vigilant for opportunities to share Islam, whether through formal settings or daily interactions.

- **Continuous Learning:** Continuously educate yourself about Islam and diverse perspectives to enrich your understanding.

METANOIA-THE REPENTANCE

- **Write and Publish:** Contribute to written media by writing articles or letters to address misconceptions or spread Islamic teachings.

- **Community Engagement:** Engage with local communities through outreach programs, social initiatives, and volunteering.

- **Seek Guidance from Scholars:** Consult knowledgeable scholars for guidance on complex theological or practical issues.

- **Reflect and Improve:** Continually reflect on your preaching efforts, seeking ways to improve and enhance your approach.

Better than a thousand days of diligent study
is one day with a great teacher.

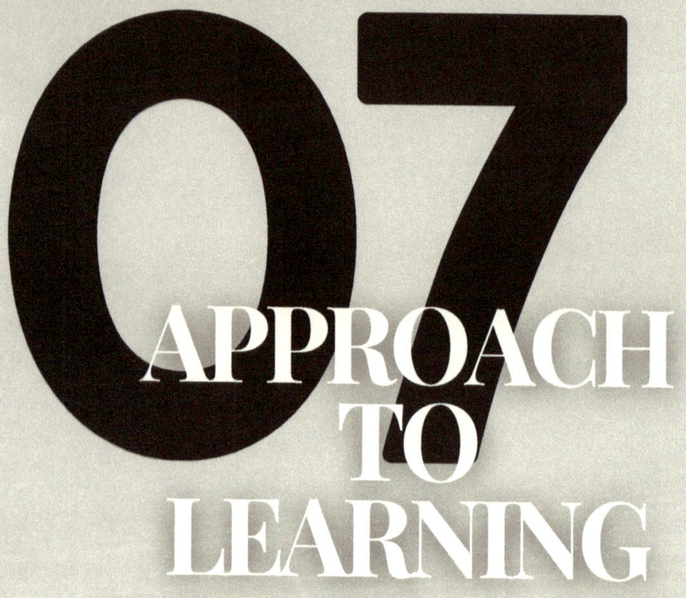
07
APPROACH
TO
LEARNING

Having a growth mindset is crucial for students as it cultivates resilience in the face of challenges, encourages persistent effort, and fosters a belief in continuous improvement. By focusing on effort and learning from setbacks, students develop a positive attitude towards learning and enhance their motivation. Embracing a growth mindset also supports a healthy self-image, promotes collaborative skills, and prepares students for future success by equipping them with essential lifelong learning abilities. Overall, it enhances academic performance and empowers students to navigate the complexities of personal and academic growth with confidence and determination.

- **Embrace Challenges:** See challenges as opportunities to learn and grow rather than obstacles.

- **Persist in Effort:** Value effort over perfection, understanding that hard work leads to improvement.

- **Learn from Setbacks:** View failures as learning experiences and opportunities for development.

- **Welcome Feedback:** See feedback as constructive guidance for improvement rather than criticism.

METANOIA-THE REPENTANCE

- **Change Self-Talk:** Shift from "I can't" to "I can't yet," emphasizing the potential for growth.

- **Cultivate Curiosity:** Stay curious and open-minded about new ideas and ways of doing things.

- **Develop Resilience:** Build resilience by bouncing back from setbacks and maintaining optimism.

- **Celebrate Progress:** Acknowledge and celebrate incremental improvements and achievements.

- **Seek Inspiration**: Learn from the success of others and use it as motivation to push forward

- **Practice Self-Reflection:** Regularly reflect on your learning journey, identifying areas for growth and improvement.

METANOIA-THE REPENTANCE

"Today is the first day of the rest of your life."

08
FORGIVENESS

In Islam, forgiveness encompasses two essential dimensions: Allah's forgiveness and human forgiveness. Allah's forgiveness is sought privately, with sincere intention and a desire for positive change in oneself. On the other hand, human forgiveness involves explicit reconciliation between individuals, addressing physical, emotional, or mental harm caused. To achieve sincere forgiveness from a psychological standpoint, several steps are recommended: firstly, acknowledging and reflecting on the incident, then recognizing personal growth and lessons learned. It's crucial to seek closure through open communication or trusted support systems. Practicing mindfulness and meditation aids in managing emotions. From an Islamic perspective, forgiveness begins with purifying intentions solely for Allah's pleasure. Making sincere du'a for oneself and others is vital, ensuring one's heart remains free from resentment. Engaging with lectures and stories of forgiveness from Islamic teachings and personal experiences strengthens resolve. Combining psychological insights and Islamic principles, forgiving others leads to inner peace, spiritual growth, and alignment with Allah's mercy.

Learning to be forgiving for the sake of Allah is a noble endeavor in Islam, emphasizing spiritual growth, inner peace, and aligning actions with divine teachings.

- **Intention Purification:** Begin with purifying your intention solely for the pleasure of Allah.

- **Reflect on Allah's Mercy:** Contemplate Allah's boundless mercy and forgiveness as a motivation to emulate these qualities.

- **Seek Allah's Guidance:** Turn to Allah in prayer (du'a) for strength and guidance in forgiving others.

- **Understand the Virtue:** Study Islamic teachings that emphasize the virtue and rewards of forgiveness.

- **Follow the Prophet's Example:** Learn from the Prophet Muhammad's (peace be upon him) forgiving nature and his forgiving of adversaries.

- **Avoid Revenge:** Remind yourself that forgiveness prevents perpetuating cycles of anger and retaliation.

- **Let Go of Ego:** Overcome pride and ego by prioritizing the act of forgiving over personal grievances.

- **Consider the Bigger Picture:** Reflect on the transient nature of worldly disputes compared to eternal rewards.

- **Practice Patience:** Cultivate patience (sabr) in dealing with emotional wounds caused by others.

- **Forgive Others' Mistakes:** Recognize that everyone makes mistakes and deserves forgiveness.

- **Be Compassionate:** Develop empathy and compassion towards those who have wronged you.

- **Communicate Graciously:** Approach reconciliation or forgiveness discussions with kindness and understanding.

- **Forgive Yourself:** Forgive yourself for past mistakes and shortcomings as part of personal growth.

- **Repel Anger with Kindness:** Respond to hurtful actions with acts of kindness and forgiveness.

- **Practice Generosity:** Be generous in forgiving others, mirroring Allah's generosity towards Hi creation.

- **Seek Spiritual Growth:** View forgiveness as a means to elevate spiritual status and draw close to Allah.

- **Avoid Holding Grudges:** Release negative emotions and grudges through forgiveness.

- **Pray for Guidance:** Pray regularly for strength and sincerity in forgiving others.

- **Learn from Adversity:** See challenges as opportunities to exercise forgiveness and grow spiritually.

- **Trust in Allah's Decree:** Accept and trust Allah's decree, knowing that forgiveness aligns with Hi divine plan.

By internalizing these points and consistently applying them in daily life, one can cultivate a forgiving heart solely for the sake of pleasing Allah and achieving spiritual fulfillment.

09
GENEROUS

Being generous is important because it embodies the essence of compassion, empathy, and selflessness that are central to Islamic teachings and universal moral values. Generosity not only benefits those in need but also purifies the heart and soul of the giver, aligning them closer to the example set by Prophet Muhammad (ﷺ), who was known for his unparalleled generosity. In Islam, acts of charity and kindness are pathways to spiritual growth and closeness to Allah. By giving generously, Muslims fulfill their duty to help others and contribute positively to society, ultimately seeking reward not only in this world but also in the Hereafter. Generosity fosters community cohesion, alleviates suffering, and reflects a deep trust in Allah's promise to multiply rewards for acts done sincerely for His sake. Thus, generosity is not merely a gesture of goodwill but a fundamental virtue that enriches both the giver and the recipient, fostering a harmonious and compassionate society.

- **Intention:** Start with the intention to please Allah and benefit others through your actions. Sincerity in intention is crucial.

- **Start Small**: Begin with small acts of kindness and charity. This could be as simple as helping someone with their groceries or offering a sincere compliment.

- **Regular Charity:** Set aside a portion of your income regularly for charitable purposes, starting with the obligatory Zakat and adding voluntary sadaqah as you are able.

- **Be Aware of Opportunities:** Keep an eye out for opportunities to help others. It could be within your family, community, or even strangers in need.

- **Utilize Skills and Time:** Offer your skills and time to volunteer for causes that resonate with you, whether it's tutoring, mentoring, or helping in community projects.

- **Educate Yourself:** Learn more about the virtues of generosity in Islam through reading, attending lectures, or studying the lives of the Prophet Muhammad and his companions.

- **Practice Gratitude:** Cultivate a mindset of gratitude for what you have, which naturally leads to a willingness to share with others.

- **Avoid Showing Off:** Keep your acts of generosity private whenever possible, as humility is key in Islam.

- **Pray for Guidance:** Seek Allah's guidance and blessings in your journey towards becoming more generous.

- **Reflect and Improve:** Regularly reflect on your progress and areas where you can improve in generosity, seeking to make it a consistent part of your life.

By incorporating these principles and actions into your daily life, you can cultivate a generous spirit aligned with Islamic teachings, benefiting both yourself and those around you.

10

TRUTHFULNESS

Being truthful holds paramount importance in Islam as it aligns with the teachings of Allah and the examples set by Prophet Muhammad (ﷺ). Truthfulness is not just about honesty in words but encompasses integrity in actions and intentions. It serves as a foundation for trust, justice, and righteousness within oneself and society. Embracing truthfulness elevates our moral character, purifies our relationships, and earns the pleasure of Allah. It leads to inner peace and contentment, as living a life based on truth ensures consistency and clarity in our thoughts and deeds. Ultimately, practicing truthfulness not only secures our place in Paradise but also enriches our lives with blessings and guidance, both in this world and the Hereafter.

- **Intention:** Begin with a sincere intention to make truthfulness a fundamental value in your life.

- **Self-Reflection:** Regularly reflect on your thoughts, words, and actions to ensure they align with truthfulness.

- **Avoid Deception:** Refrain from lying or deceiving others, regardless of the situation or consequences.

- **Courage:** Develop the courage to speak the truth even when it may be difficult or uncomfortable.

- **Accountability:** Take responsibility for your words and actions. Admit mistakes and rectify any falsehoods.

- **Seek Knowledge:** Educate yourself about the importance of truthfulness in Islam through Quranic verses and Hadith.

- **Company:** Surround yourself with truthful and righteous individuals who can support and inspire you.

- **Prayer:** Seek Allah's guidance and strength through prayer to uphold truthfulness in all aspects of life.

- **Repentance:** If you have a history of dishonesty, sincerely repent to Allah and resolve to change your ways.

- **Honesty with Yourself:** Be honest in self-assessment and acknowledge areas where improvement is needed.

- **Transparency:** Practice transparency in your interactions and ensure your actions are open and honest.

- **Consistency:** Strive for consistency in speaking the truth, making it a habit in your daily life.

- **Patience:** Develop patience in maintaining truthfulness, especially in challenging situations.

- **Guidance:** Seek advice and guidance from knowledgeable individuals or scholars on how to strengthen truthfulness.

- **Avoid Gossip:** Refrain from spreading rumors or engaging in gossip, which often involves falsehoods.

- **Mindfulness:** Be mindful of your speech. Think before you speak and ensure your words are truthful and beneficial.

- **Educate Others:** Share the virtues of honesty in Islam with others and encourage them to uphold truthfulness.

- **Humility:** Remain humble in your commitment to truthfulness, avoiding pride or self-righteousness.

- **Seek Forgiveness:** Seek forgiveness from Allah and others if you have previously been dishonest or hurtful through lies.

- **Perseverance**: Stay committed to your journey of truthfulness. Overcoming old habits and nurturing new virtues takes time and effort.

By incorporating these practices into your life with sincerity and dedication, you can strengthen your adherence to truthfulness as guided by Islamic teachings. May Allah grant you success in this endeavor.

I leave behind me two things, the Quran and the Sunnah and if you follow these you will never go astray....

FORGOTTEN SUNNAHS

SUNNAH <3

When I see Muslims deeply connected to and admiring their faith in Islam, I notice that it makes some people uncomfortable. It's equally disturbing to these individuals that many Muslims still follow the teachings of their religion despite all the temptations present in society. One tactic used to reduce Islam's influence on Muslims is to distance them from their faith under the guise of religion itself. This can be achieved in various ways. For example, some liberal scholars, who are overly impressed by the West and its culture, use a particular method. They claim: "Because people are becoming detached from religion, we are making it easier for them. By doing so, we are bringing people closer to religion. Since following the Sunnah and recommended acts (Mustahabbat) is difficult, we only discuss what is compulsory (Fard) and necessary (Wajib). We do not emphasize the importance of the Sunnah in worship and other aspects of life."

Encouraging others to follow the Sunnah of the Prophet ﷺ is important to me for many reasons. The first point I understand is that the fundamental reason for a Muslim to act upon the Sunnah is because Allah Almighty commanded us to follow the Prophet ﷺ.

The Almighty stated:

قُلْ اِنْ كُنْتُمْ تُحِبُّوْنَ اللّٰهَ فَاتَّبِعُوْنِىْ

*Say you, O Beloved; that '(O) people! If you love Allah,
you should therefore obey me.*
[Surah Aal Imran, verse 31]

Allah Almighty has also stated:

وَّ اتَّبِـعْ سَبِيْلَ مَنْ اَنَابَ اِلَىَّ-

'And follow the path of the one who has turned to Me.'
[Surah Luqman, verse 15]

The Prophet ﷺ turned to Allah Almighty the most. We
should follow him without any restrictions, which
includes following him in acts that are Fard, Wajib,
Sunnah and Mustahab.

Allah Almighty declared the life of the Prophet ﷺ an
excellent example. The Almighty states:

Indeed, for you following the Messenger of Allah is best
[Surah. Al-Ahzaab, verse 21]

Just as the Fard and Wajib acts are a part of this
perfect example, so too are the non-Wajib acts of
worship and dealings conducted by the Prophet ﷺ

METANOIA-THE REPENTANCE

The point I understand is that there is great religious wisdom behind following the Sunnah. I realize that in life, we don't just do what is necessary; we also engage in activities that help us accomplish those necessary tasks. For instance, during my educational journey, I studied books that weren't part of the syllabus. Similarly, in my profession, I not only acquired essential skills but also learned skills from other fields. I also take precautions to avoid greater problems, like wearing a jacket in freezing conditions to prevent catching a cold. In my daily life, I don't just achieve my main goals; I also go the extra mile. For example, after building a house, I decorate it with paint and choose enhancements like marble flooring. The point I'm making is that, although some actions aren't strictly necessary, they prevent negative outcomes, enhance beauty, or support the completion of necessary tasks.

Human nature dictates that a person who pays attention to small things will pay extra attention to related things that are of greater importance. It is not the case that someone who avoids doubtful things unreluctantly commits things that are definitively haram. This wisdom has been alluded to in the Hadith that states a person grazing his animals near the field of the king will find his animals entering the field. Hence, it is safer to avoid even the boundary of such a thing lest one falls into that which is actually forbidden. Adopting this careful approach will act as a barrier whereby something unprohibited prevents you from accessing that which is prohibited.

METANOIA-THE REPENTANCE

From my personal experience, I was a kid who thought that when I grow up, I would keep a beard, thinking it was just a sunnah and not a big deal. But then, by Allah's will, I changed my mind and started growing a beard, not realizing it would change my whole life. Initially, it was just some hairs on my face that meant nothing to me. But slowly, I changed my ways and came closer to deen because of the beard, which was not intentional. I started seeing changes that I hadn't even anticipated. The point I am trying to explain is that following just one sunnah can bring you so much closer to Islam in ways you never imagined, and in the best way possible.

At times, it is fascinating how actions that are optional and Mustahab act as a more effective barrier stopping sins than a barrier premised on actions that are necessary. For example, a person may wear a turban—which is a Sunnah of the Prophet ﷺ or have a shawl over his head—which is the custom of the pious people. Such a person will not go to the pub wearing this attire as it will stop him from doing so. Even if he was to go, he would first leave this Sunnah by changing into shirt and trousers or some other clothing and then go. It is not plausible that a bearded Muslim will wear a turban or topi and go to the pub. Note how a Sunnah and Mustahab act can prevent someone from the impermissible act of going to a pub.

Not only this, but we also observe in society that if a bearded shopkeeper with a turban who, suppose, deceives whilst selling goods, people will make remarks like: i) 'Brother, how can you do such things despite being religious?' ii) 'How can you do such things despite having a beard?' iii) 'How can you wear a turban and do such things?'

Looking at another example, if a person wearing a turban sits down and converses with people at the time of Salah and does not get up to go and pray, even those who do not pray themselves will say: 'The azan has taken place and Salah is taking place in congregation. So, go and pray Salah.' It is almost as if his turban—a Sunnah—is compelling him to pray Salah. What is the takeaway from all these examples? Acts that are Sunnah and Mustahab are perceived by others as a barrier that prevents sin.

Another aspect of acts that are Sunnah is that they beautify righteous deeds. For example, it is compulsory to wear clothing that covers a person from the navel to below the knees. However, to cover the entire body is Sunnah, which also looks more presentable. Likewise, one can eat and drink whilst walking, but eating whilst respectfully seated is more refined. In a similar manner, when meeting someone, a person can start a conversation and get straight to point without offering any respectful greeting. However, this would be considered discourteous.

Conversely, initiating a meeting with salaam is
Sunnah, and it is also Sunnah to smile if appropriate.
Both things add to the amiability of the meeting.
Specific units (Rak'aat) are Fard in Salah, but the
Sunnahs in the beginning and end enhance one's focus
in Salah and increase closeness to Allah Almighty.
Similarly, Hajj is Fard, but performing Sunnah Umrahs
throughout life immerse you in divine love. The Fard
fasts of Ramadan are a means of attaining piety, but
observing Sunnah fasts from time-to-time throughout
the year helps in maintaining this state of piety.

In summary, it is necessary for us to do whatever is
Fard and Wajib and to stay away from haram.
However, we should not leave out acts of Sunnah in
the process. Rather, we should act upon them too as
they help us to fulfil and beautify that which is Fard
and avoid sins.

THE OBLIGATION AND AWESOME REWARD FOR REVIVNG A SUNNAH

It is reported that Imām Al-Zuhrī – Allāh have mercy on him – said:

Those of our scholars who went before us used to say,"Adherence to the Sunnah is salvation, but knowledge is taken away quickly, so the revival of knowledge means the stability of religion and worldly affairs, and the loss of knowledge means the loss of all that."

The Prophet (صلى الله عليه وسلم) said: Ahead of you there lie days of patience, during which being patient will be like grasping a hot coal. The one who does good deeds then will have a reward like that of fifty men who do such deeds. And someone else added: They said: Oh Messenger of Allaah, the reward of fifty of them? He said: The reward of fifty of you.

 In some reports of the hadeeth, it reads, **"They are the ones who will revive my Sunnah and teach it to the people."** (Narrated by Abu Dawood (4341); al-Tirmidhi (3085) and he said: it is a hasan hadeeth. It was classed as saheeh by al-Albaani in al-Silsilah al-Saheehah [494])

Thawbaan stated that the Messenger of Allah ﷺ said, "There will always remain a group from my Ummah steadfast and manifest upon the truth. They are unharmed by those who desert them, and they will remain like this until the order of Allah is established."

The Best of the Muslims Revive the Sunnah

Yusef ibn Rayhaan said: My father told me: I heard Abu 'Abdillaah Muhammad ibn Isma'eel (Bukhaaree) say: The best of the Muslims is a man who revives a Sunnah from the Sunnah of the Messenger that had died. So be patient oh people of the Sunnan, may Allah have mercy on you, for indeed you are the minority among the people. [Al-Jaami' Li Akhlaaq Ar-Raawee Wa Aadaab As-Saami' of Al-Khateeb Al-Baghdaadee vol. 1, p. 168, Muasasah Ar-Risaalah]

FORGOTTEN SUNNAHS WE SHOULD PRACTICE DAILY

1. WAKING UP AND CLEARING YOUR NOSE

Prophet Muhammad ﷺ said,
"When one of you wakes up from his sleep, he must blow of his nose three times, for the shaytan spends the night inside one's nostrils."
(Al-Bukhari and Muslim)

2. AVOID BLOWING OR EXHALING BREATH INTO YOUR DRINK

It is narrated in the hadith below:
"Do not blow from your mouth into food and water."
(Bukhari)
Additionally, science proves that you carry some of the bacteria in your mouth, and by blowing it on food or drinking water you are transferring all of the bacteria into your drink or food too. The carbon dioxide that we exhale can also decrease the number of blood pH in our bodies.

3. DRINK IN 3 GULPS!

The Prophet ﷺ said,
"Do not drink in one breath just as the camel does. Rather, drink twice and thrice, and mention (Allah's) Name before drinking and thank (Him) upon finishing." (Bukhari & Muslim)

The Prophet ﷺ would not gulp His drink down in one go, rather He ﷺ would take three sips and breathe in between each one, and did not breathe into the vessel from which He ﷺ was drinking.

It is recommended to sit down when you drink, take breaks as you drink instead of gulping it down and saying Alhamdulillah after. Drinking water in a rush will cause more harm than good, as it can also cause choking.

4. HAVE A DRINK OF WATER AFTER DRINKING MILK

The Prophet ﷺ drank some milk then called for some water. Once He ﷺ got the water, He ﷺ rinsed His mouth and said:

It has fat. (Al-Bukhari and Muslim)

Imam An-Nawawi said in Sharh Saheeh Muslim: This hadith confirms it's recommended to rinse the mouth after drinking milk.

5. DON'T SAY YUCK

Abu Huraira reported:

The Messenger of Allah ﷺ would never complain about food. If He ﷺ liked something, He ﷺ would eat it. If He ﷺ disliked it, He ﷺ would leave it. (Bukhari & Muslim)

Sometimes, we might be guilty of taking things for granted. Hence, we should always remember to be grateful, and to never complain about our blessings and rezeki.

6. SMILING TO OTHERS

The Prophet ﷺ said: "Your smiling in the face of you
brother is charity.." Hasan (At-Tirmidhi)
The easiest charity that does not involve money is t
smile at others. Smiling is contagious and it can ligh
up someone else's day. Your brain release
neuropeptides, dopamine, serotonin, and endorphin
when you smile. These molecules fight stress, reliev
pain, and act as antidepressants. A smile will benefi
everyone who sees it, and even those who don't smil
will end up smiling as a result.

7. ALWAYS SEEK FORGIVENESS FROM ALLAH S.W.T

Whether we realise it or not, human nature always ha
a tendency to sin. Thus, we are encouraged to alway
say astaghfirullah hal adzim, to seek forgiveness fron
Allah S.W.T, even when we don't feel like we hav
recently sinned. Allah's forgiveness lifts the burden o
sins that prevent your prayers from being accepted
and keeps our hearts at ease.
The knowledge that is at our fingertips allows us t
start with the simple act of sunnahs among many. W
should start with these sunnah and slowly get used t
them, and then continuously strive for improvement
adding more sunnah to our daily routine.

8. Using the miswak before every prayer.

The Messenger of Allah ﷺ has said: "Were it not that I would be overburdening my community I would have ordered them to use a tooth-stick." (Mawatah Malik)

9. Walking barefoot

Sayyiduna Abdullah Ibn Buraydah reported: "Rasulullah ﷺ commanded us to walk barefoot (Occasionally)." [Abu Dawud]

10. Eating from the side of the plate

Rasulullaha ﷺ said, "Blessing descends upon the middle of the food, so eat from the sides of the plate (which is nearest to you) and do not eat from the middle." (Abu Dawud)

11. Doing cupping (hijama)

On the authority of Anas bin Malik-May Allah be pleased with him-said that the Prophet ﷺ said: The best treatment which you get is cupping. (Muslim)

12. Sitting and drinking

Sayyiduna Anas Ibn Maalik reported that Rasulullah ﷺ prevented them from standing and drinking. [Sahih Muslim]

13. Sleeping in the state of Wudhu

Rasululah ﷺ said, " There is no person who goes to sleep in a state of Wudhu but an Angel spends the night with him, and every time he turns over, the Angel says, O Allah! forgive Your slave, for he went to bed in a state of Wudhu. ®[AlMuJamAlAwsat]

14. Greeting children

Sayyiduna Anas narrates that whenever Rasulullah ﷺ would pass by young children, He ﷺ would greet them. [Sahih Bukhari]

15. Reciting the 3 Quls

Sayyidah Aisha RA narrates, "Whenever Rasulullah ﷺ went to bed at night, he would join His hands, blow into them(after) reciting Surahs Ikhlaas, Falaq and Naas and then pass his hands over his body starting with his face and head, He would do this thrice." (Sahih Bukhari)

16. Dua while wearing a new dress

When Messenger of Allah ﷺ wore a new garment, He would name it. For instance, a turban or shirt or cloak and would supplicate:
"O Allah, all the praise is for You that You have given it to me to put on. I ask You its goodness and the goodness of the purpose for which it was made,

and I seek Your Protection from its evil and the evil of the purpose for which it was made." [Abu Dawud and At-Tirmidhi].

17. Making Dua for Others

Rasulullah ﷺ said, "No Muslim makes Dua for another Muslim in his absence except that the
angels say: 'May the same be for you too."
(Sahih Muslim)

18. Writing a will.

"It is not right for a Muslim who has anything concerning which a will should be made, to abide for more than three nights without having a written will with him." (An Nisai)

19. Dusting the bed before going to sleep

Rasulullah ﷺ said, "When any one of you goes to bed, he should first dust it and say 'Bismillah' because he does not know what might have entered (the bed)."
(Sahih Muslim)

20. Picking up and eating food that has fallen on the ground

Rasulullah ﷺ said, "Whenever a morsel falls then pick it up, clean it, eat it and do not leave it for Shaytaan".

He ﷺ also commanded us to lick the plate saying, You do not know in which morsel lies the Barakah (blessings)" (Sahih Muslim)

21. Getting wet in the rain.

Anas May Allah be pleased with him said: It rained upon us as we were with the Messenger of Allah ﷺ. Rasulullah ﷺ removed his cloth (from a part of his body) till the rain fell on it. We said: Messenger of Allah ﷺ, why did you do this? He ﷺ said: It is because it (the rainfall) has just come from the Exalted Lord. (Muslim)

There are two words which are light on the tongue, heavy on the scale, and loved by the Most Merciful: SubhanAllahi wa bihamdi, SubhanAllahi al-azeem (Glorified is Allah and praised is He, Glorified is Allah the Most Great).
(Bukhari and Muslim)

سُبْحَانَ اللّٰهِ وَ بِحَمْدِهِ ، سُبْحَانَ اللّٰهِ العَظِيم

Suggestions for further reading...

If you're looking for your next inspiring read, here are four books that I highly recommend:

1. Ikigai: The Japanese Secret to a Long and Happy Life - Discover the Japanese concept of Ikigai, which means "a reason for being." This book combines philosophy, psychology, and practical advice to help you find your own ikigai and live a more fulfilling life.

2. Atomic Habits: An Easy & Proven Way to Build Good Habits & Break Bad Ones - A must-read for anyone looking to make lasting changes in their life. James Clear provides actionable strategies to form good habits, break bad ones, and master the tiny behaviors that lead to remarkable results.

METANOIA-THE REPENTANCE

3. Motivational Muslims - This book is a treasure trov
of quotes and insights from successful Muslir
individuals who have made a significant impact ii
their respective fields. Their journeys are not onl;
motivational but also deeply rooted in their faith
providing a unique perspective on achieving success.

4. Life Towards Allah - A profound exploration o
spiritual growth and the journey towards a close
relationship with Allah. This book delves into th
practical steps one can take to strengthen their fait
and live a life that is pleasing to the Creator.

These books offer a blend of spiritual growth
practical advice, and motivational stories that ca
help guide you on your journey towards a mor
meaningful and fulfilling life. Happy reading!

NOTES

METANOIA-THE REPENTANCE

NOTES

HOW TO MAKE A CORNER BOOKMARK

1- Cut out the corner bookmark.
2- Fold up your bookmark, so you end up with a square.
3- Glue the two back pieces together.
4- Trim any excess overlap to have a nice square.
5- Enjoy!

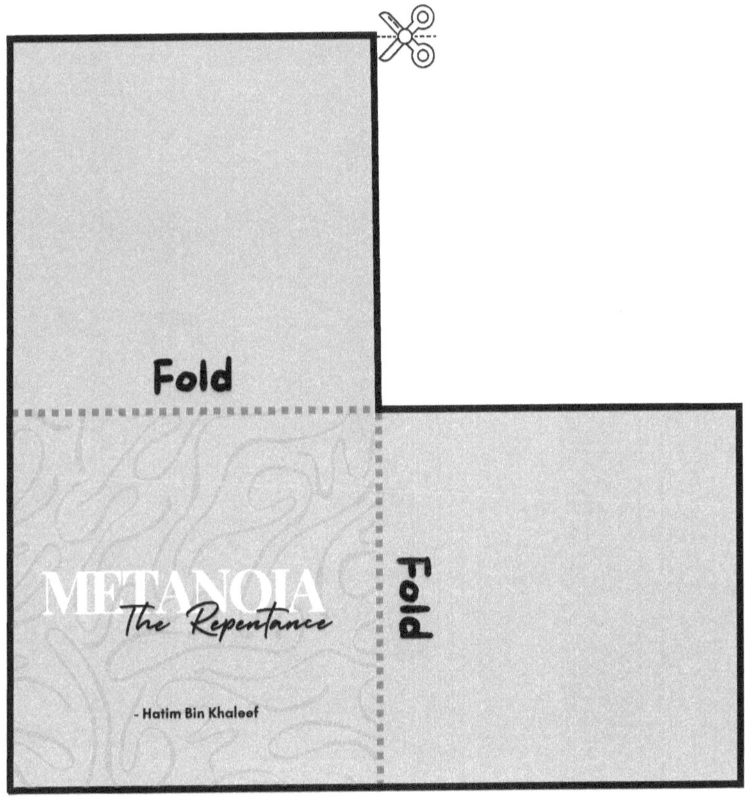